In The Margins Of The World

Willa Schneberg

[signature]

FOR JENNIFER,
WHO KNEW ME WHEN
OCT 07

Plain View Press
P. O. 33311
Austin, TX 78764

plainviewpress.com
sbright1@austin.rr.com
1-800-878-3605

1

Cover photo by Willa Schneberg.
Author photo by Kevin Forg.

Also by Willa Schneberg

Box Poems, Alice James Books

To Bette Mandl who always believed in my poetry,
to my mother who taught me to love to read,
and to Robin, for everything.

Acknowledgments

"Genuine Imitation": Maryland Poetry Review;
"Chiropractic School": Southern Poetry Review;
"Darkest Africa": Permafrost;
"Harem": Sing Heavenly Muse; Poems in Praise of the Arabic Woman;
"Dogwoods At Forty-One": Sow's Ear;
Each in Her Own Way: Women Writing About the Menopause (anthology) Queen of Swords Press;
Claiming the Spirit Within (anthology) Beacon Press;
"When The Moon Hides": Arab / Muslim Issue, Mr.Cogito Press;
"Not The Lecture": Bridges: A Journal for Jewish Feminists And Our Friends;
"Kaddish For Felix Nussbaum (1904-1944)": Bridges: A Journal...;
Passionate Lives: Eight Autobiographical Poem Cycles (anthology) Queen of Swords Press;
Beyond Lament: Poets of the World Bearing Witness to the Holocaust (anthology) Northwestern University Press;
"The Dybbuk Searches For A Home": Cincinnati Judaica Review;
"Strolling With Solomon Ibn Gabirol And Judah Ha-Levi": Exquisite Corpse; Passionate Lives ...
"Simchas Torah, Satmar Synagogue": Cincinnati Judaica Review; The Jewish Calendar 5754;
"For Hashem": Cincinnati Judaica Review;
"To Expand Freely In The Margin Of The World": Poems in Praise of the Arabic Woman;
 Salmon Magazine; Willamette Week;
"Bedding Down": Women's Review of Books; Hard Love: Writings on Violence and Intimacy (anthology) Queen of Swords Press;
"My Father's Tour Of East New York": Women's Review of Books; Passionate Lives...;
"Porno Drive-In, Knoxville, TN": Tikkun; Tikkun- The Anthology;
"Three Way Conversation": Sifrut; Israel Horizons; Bridges: A Journal ...: Passionate Lives...   ;
"Spilled Milk": Sojourner; Passionate Lives...;
"Expanded/Extended Memory": Bridges: A Journal....;
"One Friday At The Katz's": Bridges: A Journal ....;
"Pick-Up Sticks": Sow's Ear;
"Army Brat": Americas Review;
"A Tunnel Like Any Other": Psychopoetica;
"The Oral Tradition": Bridges: A Journal...;
"Collect Call From A Pay Phone In A Maon Olim": Bridges: A Journal...;
"I Could Die Now": Black Buzzard Review;
"Wedding in Beersheva": Bridges: A Journal...;
"Suicide Note": Black Rose;
"Hang-Gliding": Cincinnati Judaica Review;
"Wooden Bird": Permafrost;
"The Commuter Dreams Of Bertha": The Industrial Worker;
"Big Red": Embers;
"Biscuits": Z Miscellaneous;
"A Visit To The Bible Belt After Eight Years": Jewish Women's Literary Annual, different version;
"A Thousand And One Nights": Maryland Poetry Review;
"Other Side Of The Coin": Vergin Press;
"Expatriate": Hawaii Pacific Review; Studio Potter;
"My Father Leaves The Hospital Wearing His Yellow Shirt": Israel Horizons;
"Conch Republic": Emrys Journal;
"Staying Put": Poets' On; The Oregonian;
"Staying Put" was awarded the Erika Mumford Prize For Poetry;
"A Visit To The Bible Belt After Eight Years" was awarded Second Prize in the
 Allen Ginsberg Poetry Award Competition;
"To Expand Freely In The Margin Of The World" was awarded Second Prize for Poetry in the Willamette Week Writers' Contest.

Thanks to:
Thanks to Literary Arts, Inc., whose fellowships greatly helped in the completion of this book, and to the MacDowell Colony and the Corporation of Yaddo, who gave me time.

Special thanks to Hannah Stein and Ruth Gundle who helped shape this manuscript and to the Pearl Poets for their feedback and commitment to the craft.

Contents

I

II

III

I

Genuine Imitation

Give me the fake,
the imitation, the simulation, any day
over the real thing.
Give me the bronze garbage
in Haymarket Square
with the inlaid crumpled Boston Globe,
embedded lettuce leaves,
flattened fish scales,
that will never be burned,
bagged or rotted.
Give me the plaster life size cows
black with white spots
shaped like clouds,
in the parking lot outside
the Hilltop Steak House,
who will not experience
the irritation of flies or
the teat sucking machine.
Give me my daughter's model trains
endlessly circling towns
that have no pollution,
everyone's welcome and whoever's
sick goes to the doll hospital.
Give me the poem,
its room not even a page wide,
where one enters as often as one likes
to watch the man place quarters
on his dead wife's lids,
to feel the grief not your own.

Chiropractic School

I'm learning how to palpate,
to feel coins through my pants pockets,
to know the difference between
a quarter—its eagle's wings spread full
and the coin with Susan B. Anthony's
determined profile, and to feel
the texture of one of my grey hairs
beneath twenty-five sheets of the Yellow Pages.

You will never know how my fingers
could cure you
before you realize you are ill.

While you grind your teeth
without me to massage your tight jaw loose
and dream of pushing open your coffin's lid,
I open my bone box
to touch an ilium and ischium
so gently they stay asleep,
forgetting they ever lived
trapped in a body.

Darkest Africa

for Tex

I loved the moss-haired girl, never cared to look
in the medicine cabinet to see if she had any
bottled green liquid, never wanted to touch her hair
out of fear that it wasn't springy-soft. I first saw
her in the freak tent sitting in front of a forest
back-drop, and spoke to her when I offered
her a glass of my pink lemonade for nothing, since
it was so hot and the sweat snaked down her temples.
Before, I tried selling balloons, but never felt right
tacking them so I could sell more, I even apprenticed
with the knife swallower, until I learned that he
held them in his throat and kept good farmers'
knives to hock later. But the moss-haired girl
said she wouldn't marry me, if I barked lemonade
for the rest of my life, so I put on spangled pink
tights, got into the center ring to understand how
lions are like sheep, if one jumps over you all the
rest will follow, but the whip and pistol even filled
with blanks made me jumpy from power I did not
deserve and I didn't like the crowd the way I used to,
knowing that when I opened the lion's mouth wide
and stuck my head in, they wished for the worst.
After we tied the knot, the moss-haired girl started
hanging her wig on a hook and sleeping bald and I
would spend more and more time with Helena, the
gorilla, who McKay trained to wear stockings with
garters and to pour tea so well that Stoke-on-Trent,
England designed a tea set especially for her. And
night after night we would scheme how I would
spring her and take her home to darkest Africa.

Harem

for Hudda Shaarawi (1879-1947), first to remove the veil in Egypt

Wooden lattice screens cover the windows
we sit behind. No one
who stands in the street
can see us.

In the paddock,
in the kraal,
in the mew
we are you,
except your day will come.

Horse, you will see your shadow in the pink desert.
Turtle, you will find your reflection in the sea.
Hawk, you will leave your claw marks
on the necks of chickens.

We are the stale in tins,
the brine choked in barrels,
the jaundice in eggs.

It is true that sometimes the eunuchs let us out,
but we never escape;
covered completely in black cloth
we carry picnic baskets in our gloved hands
and in our eyes... daggers.

Sunday Service

I watch the sisters of the church
dressed in white.
Some wear the same uniforms
they work in five days a week
as nurses aides. They fan themselves
with heavy pieces of cardboard
attached to popsicle sticks
on one side advertising Sawyer's Mortuary,
on the other Jackson's Grave Monuments.
Soon they will leap to their feet,
sway from side to side,
clap their hands for Jesus.

A sax backs up the preacher:
Jesus went to a desert place and found
a Well of Love. Yes he did! Yes he did—
a Well of Love, brothers and sisters.
I tell you brothers and sisters, the well
of love is Here, right Here in Knoxville!
Yes, brothers and sisters, JE-SUS
is the Lord of Knoxville,
HAL LE LU JAH   HA LE LU JAH!

The woman next to me is crying,
her wide bosom heaving,
her thick legs stomping as she shouts out,
Praise the Lord, Hallelujah, Praise the Lord!,
her faith tangible as her car payments,
while I sit, my arms folded across my chest,
wishing the spirit would overtake me
and I would hear myself wailing,
Save me Jesus, Save Me!

Dogwoods At Forty-One

Although her period is heavy as usual
and requires two tampons and a pad,
she pauses this time
before flushing
the blood-clotted cotton
down the commode to watch the red
dye the water.

At forty-one she is surprised
she is happy with her queasy stomach
and swollen breasts,
although she never wanted children.

Now it is not enough for her
to observe dogwoods profuse
with pink and white petals
from her window,
she must take them inside,
filling every glass in the house
with their short-lived beauty.

When The Moon Hides

Turkey became a republic in 1924. Soon, wearing of
traditional headgear was forbidden, polygamy prohibited
and spoken or written Arabic outlawed.

I was never like the other eunuchs
who dangled their preserved members
in silk sacks around their necks. Long ago
I stopped wishing I were a pruned jade plant
that would again grow full and forest
the chamber of the Sultan's favorite odalisque,
the Circassian with ivory skin.

But I will never find myself
in Ataturk's new Turkey where
my turban has become a partridge nest,
the muezzin calls only in memory
and my beloved Koranic script that whirled
across the page is beheaded.

As we dressed the favored ones in damask pants
brocaded with silver flowers and touched
the bejeweled faces peasants will never glimpse,
or when they betrayed us and
we loaded them on rowboats
stuffed in sacks,
to be sacrificed to the watery depths,
power seeped from my phantom phallus.

Now, I do not go out except on nights
when the moon hides.
I walk by the Bosphorus and watch
the ones who know fish
fry their catch in oil.
My ebony skin tightens against my bones.
I am almost invisible
to the fishermen who offer me
fish heads and fish scales.

Not The Lecture

Emma Goldman and Ben Reitman were engaged
in a torrid love affair from 1908 - 1917

Hobo of the flowing silk ties,
the subject of this evening is not
Variety or Monogamy — Which?, since
you'll never understand the supreme
difference between love given freely
and promiscuity anyway, and I
have become the love slave that watches
passively as your apparition,
that sometime crusader for the unemployed,
takes up every seat in the union hall,
transforming each face in the audience
into your face; so to give the lecture
Jealousy — Its Causes and Possible Cure,
I have to look over your heads and pretend
I am the old Emma content to curl up
with the Sab Cat, because your new Emma,
born from loving you is a traitor
to her own words and almost wishes
for San Diego again, the free speech fight,
the vigilantes burning I.W.W. on your rump,
tarring and rubbing sagebrush all over
your weak-fleshed body.
You feed on innocent love-starved girls
in flea-trap hotels, as I hold
thousands in the palm of my hand, but
I still want only your Willie in my Treasure Box.
Hobo, you handsome devil, lie down next to me.
I'm learning how to be your mother, sister,
daughter, woman of your dreams,
so when your billy club begins to rise
for another and you stare at her again
above the breasts, you'll find my blue eyes
looking through you.

Kaddish For Felix Nussbaum (1904 - 1944)

The German Jewish painter Felix Nussbaum died in Auschwitz.

I

Strapped in my life,
like breasts in a brassiere,
I couldn't get to you
although I tried.
The Women's Army Auxiliary Corps
said I was too young to go overseas,
so they sent me to Fort Benning
to stand at attention saluting
until the savage sun would
topple me like a dreidel.

So sorry for myself
while you were behind electrified
barbed wire in St. Cyprien,
either sweltering in cement barracks
or scorched, the sun never
ceasing its beating,
you sleeping on sand and straw,
your plate a tin can. But somehow you kept painting
tallised men entering a makeshift synagogue,
their backs to the horror and yourself
surrounded by walls impossible to climb,
wearing the yellow star on your coat
and holding a Jewish identity card;
so I could go to Chattanooga on leave,
dance the lindy with *sheigitz* boys,
eat a B.L.T. for the first time
and visit a plastic surgeon
to have my nose made non-Jewish,
small and turned-up.

II

Yes, you and Felka hid together
in Brussels at Rue Archimede,
but you never loved her.
You saw her through the eyes
in the back of your head and heard her
only faintly over the din behind

whatever you spoke or thought,
the stomping up the stairs,
the fist pounding the door.
If you were with me
you would not have painted the vase
with the stem bent in half,
or you two in a stiff embrace
as if chained together.
In my body you would have returned
to your summers in Norderney
and afterwards we would be
a small blue boat slightly rocking.

III

If I could have taken you back
to my old neighborhood in Brooklyn,
where Uncle Dave had the only car
and we all piled in, you probably
wouldn't have become a painter
"who spoke for an entire generation
of artists who were exiled, hunted,
banned or imprisoned" and I would
never have seen you in a museum
and fallen in love
with your taut, determined face.
At best, you might have become a fine arts
professor painting your mother solid
in a flowered dress and yourself

Continued

at the easel in a pink-lit
country road near Osnabruck,
where you were young; and at worst,
which really isn't so bad,
you might have given up painting altogether
and taken a desk job like my Irving,
who went with me and the kids
every Sunday, July and August
to the beach at Coney Island to hear
transistors blaring, the ice-cream man
chanting, "dixie cups, popsicles."

The Dybbuk Searches For A Home

I

The Dybbuk Speaks

When I slept, I knew my soul
left my body and traveled
to places on the opposite side of the world,
regions with names I could not even pronounce,
provinces the elders told me
I had no business knowing,
but now when its neither day nor night,
I am no longer allowed to wear my body.
It is covered over with earth outside my village,
veined rocks on the tombstone and
I am way up like a flying machine or
a dirigible above toothpick bridges,
birdbath ponds and the cacophony. It
never gets here where stars prick the sky
and I hear my own thoughts circling.

Why didn't I stop myself from reading
those profane books? The last day
in my dark room the great rabbis came to me
holding before them copies of the holy *Shulhan Arukh*.
Lightning bolts shot out of those tomes stabbing
my words vibrating with Spinoza, Sabbeti Zvi,
Virginia Woolf, whose letters changed and rearranged
themselves into new meanings over the heads
of the *tzaddiks* petrified to consider that what
they knew to be true may be false.

Why did I have to wear men's clothes and slip
into the taverns of the farm boys from Radymishal
to slap coins on bar counters on Shabbos

Continued

and listen to them talk about taking girls against
their will and pressing back fingers in brawls?
If only it were not too late

and I was not doomed to invade bodies,
I would be able to sleep and be Tzeena
who has one child in diapers
and one in her belly.

II

The One Possessed Speaks

This cannot be happening to me.
My hands paralyzed by my sides.
My lips not moving and
a woman's voice coming out of my mouth.

Every Friday afternoon I wait at the bus station
for the soldier boys
who see cinema on Shabbos,
to strap the holy leather boxes
on their left arms
and above their eyes and cajole
these dissolute souls to bind with our G-d
for even a split second
before resuming their deluded lives.

I would never dream of eating
before washing my hands
and saying the *barucha*. But my wife, Rivka
whose brain is the size of a macaroon,
glory be to G-d, sometimes lights
the candles from the wrong direction
and makes soup that tastes like
a chicken flapping its wings
struggling to escape.

I try to call out to Rivka to get a doctor,
but instead a voice like a flute cries out
sobbing, "Forgive me Hashem, forgive me."
My wife slumps over in the doorway suddenly
drained of blood as if ritually slaughtered.

Just a mix-up. A squatter was looking for a frog
or a goy and got lost in my body.

I slapped my wife only once and only
when I found hidden behind volumes
of the *Mishnah*, a profane book,
not Brothers Karamazov mind you,
but a cheap paperback. On the cover
a girl in a slinky dress
runs past a castle in a storm.

I try to burp or fart out the freeloader,
but its crochet hooks jab in deeper,
as it whines, "I'll never find peace, never."

Not to worry, I tell myself.
The rabbis are on the way to say the verses
backwards and forwards to release the scourge
and watch it hiss and spew out
between the nail and skin of the toe
ready to violate another.

Where are they?
They should be here by now...
Every Shabbos lunch there is always
at least one *shnorer* at my table and afterwards
as the High One commands I go into my wife,
who must be receiving pleasure too,
since she keeps her legs open.

Strolling With Solomon Ibn Gabriol And Judah Ha-Levi

Despite the fact they lived in Spain a thousand years ago and
she can't chat with them in Arabic or Hebrew, they are catching up. She
walks between them holding the curve of each poet's arm. The men
know each other by reputation only and are glad to finally meet in this
park enclosed by a fence of black pomegranates sculptured in wrought
iron. She tells Judah, who keeps his eyes downcast, that she made it
to Israel, the Jews are in power, Hagar's children aren't too happy, the
food is terrible, always tomatoes and cucumbers cut up small, soldiers
take every seat of the *Egged* buses and sometimes they want your
seat for their feet and rifles. She wants to lift up his chin and kiss him
on the cheek, but thinks, better not, he has his Jerusalem, a rose-shaped
spice box that will never wilt. Solomon sighs, he would have given his
life to go there, but illness made travel impossible. She explains, if he
had gallstones now, they could be cut out and he could feel God's will
big as apples leave his body. Solomon sighs again, fiddles with his *tzitzit*
replies quietly that the Lord, glory be to He who never left his side,
showed love through pain.

Alone in the park, her companions back in history, her hands are cold
in her pockets. In a moment silent as stars she yells at the heavens,
Will you ever come to my party and leave even a small sign behind,
like a Tetley tea bag that forever brews tea dark?

*Solomon Ibn Gabirol and Judah Ha-Levi were Jewish poets living in Spain in the eleventh
century. They wrote in Hebrew. Solomon Ibn Gabirol was a philosopher and as a poet was best
known for his liturgical poems. Judah Ha- Levi is considered by many to be the greatest of all
post-biblical Hebrew poets. Many of his poems deal with journeying to the Holy Land.*

24

Simchas Torah, Satmar Synagogue

(Zefat, Israel, 1988)

She sits with the other women in the tiny balcony
and does not draw attention to herself
since she now dresses as they do
sleeves covering her elbows, her hair tied back,
though she is unscarfed, yet to be married.

She tries to turn the pages,
but cannot stop fiddling
with the Jewish star
on the gold chain inside her blouse.
The words in the *siddur* on her lap
have become too heavy.

She wants to be downstairs
inside the circle of blue flame
dancing with the men
wearing silk sashed coats and wide fur hats,
so far gone on wine and Torah
they will board a train that
whips around hairpin turns in the sky
as they lean out the windows
arms flailing, trying
to touch His chariot.

Instead, she is exhausted from running behind.
The coal smoke chokes,
as she tries to catapult into the air,
knowing that no matter how high she gets
they will never extend their hands
and pull her on board.

For Hashem

On my underpants is a red stain
big as a *shekel*. I am happy
because the special time has begun
when I must sing silently
in front of my husband and
our hands may not touch.
Even passing Asher
the container of coarse salt excites me
as the air between our fingers vibrates.

Because *Hashem* has asked me to discipline
my hands and not pour water
over Asher's palms this *Shabbos*
or twirl his curly *pais* with my finger
when we lie down in the same bed tonight,
I joyfully obey.

But it still feels forever
before I will be able to remove my rings
and bobby pins and the tangles in my hair,
so the *mikvah's* waters can cling
to every follicle of me, pronouncing me ready,
more than ready for my husband.

On *Yom Chamishi*, while our children sleep,
Asher will break out the champagne
and with the lightest touch of his fingertips
find the areolas of my breasts and feel awe.

To Expand Freely In The Margin Of The World

On Oct. 7, 1901 Slimene Ehnni married Isabelle Eberhardt in Marseilles.

My wife wanted beyond what there is.
In Geneva before I knew her, her pen name
was Nicholas Podolinsky. In Toulon
dressed as a workman in a blue linen jacket,
trousers and cap, she would drink
with the sailors and pick a dark-eyed rowdy
to take into a back alley and reveal her sex.

We met in Algeria. I was a cavalry sergeant
in the colonial regiment. Regal on my mount
wearing a red *spahi* cloak and tight black boots
I almost believed I was a Frenchman, but Isabelle
was Moslem, fasting on *Ramadan* until the sun
stretched out and snored over the mud domes of El Oued.
She knew every salutation and pious exclamation
in my language as if her knees and palms
always prostrated themselves to Allah.

Forced to rendezvous clandestinely,
I would watch her gallop across the scrub
her small body lost in a burnoose,
its hood flapping. Arriving without a word
she would leap off her stallion towards the well
and plunge her shaved head into the cold water.

Before long she is Si Mahoud,
the young Turk on holiday from university,
who smokes *kief* with legionnaires in brothels
splendid with Sudanese beauties and soon disappears
to visit desert lizards, the nomads of Morocco
whose jewels are guns and powder,
until the bout with malaria
reminds her she is a woman
trembling under a camel's hair blanket,

Continued

delirious in a great dark tent.
He wanted to make love without responsibility,
to feel the absence of death's fingers in cometary moments
of love-making, but *she* loved me.
We embraced on the blue woolen mattress
on the stone floor, my revolver next to us.

Being half the man Si Mahoud was,
never brilliant nor free, Isabelle chose *him*.
I was already dead to her in Ain Sefra,
when the wadis' yellow waters
swept her away with the rubbish and the trees.

II

Bedding Down

Yippie! it's time for the egg cups
to lie on the their sides,
the knives flat on their backs,
the cards neat in their decks
in the kitchen drawer,
for the window's big eye
to flirt with the moon and for
the two who undress in that room
not to fight or bemoan what
they didn't do today
or need to do tomorrow,
but to climb in nude as olives
between flannel sheets
and fit together like a teaspoon
and tablespoon measuring nothing.

My Father's Tour Of East New York

Willa, look out the window— that boarded up
building at the corner of Livonia and Wyona is
where Izzy Bedrock used to live as a boy,
the one who became a dentist and ate himself
to death. See that tall building coming
up on your side. They broke the window of
their own church. That was the shul where I
was bar-mitzvahed. It wasn't a money-making
operation then, like it is for kids nowadays.
I read the *Havtorah*. The women were home setting
out the gefilte fish, the *challah*, the sponge cake
for the few relatives who could come to share
my father's *nachus*. Look at this rubble. It was
Blake Avenue— a thriving shopping street lined
with stores and pushcarts selling fruit, nuts,
tsiz-tsiz, scrubbing boards, ribbons, chicken
for Friday night. I bought there my first pair of
long pants. Two blocks down, the right hand
side—stick your hand out the window—is
what remains of the magnificent Premier. Matinees
were only a dime. When your mother was still
all sweetness and light, she and I would spend
a Sunday afternoon there.

Black kids rollerskate in the street. My father
honks. They don't move out of the way. They won't
defy me, my father says. He drives towards them
as if they are pins and he is a bowling ball.
A hairsbreath away from the smallest kid, he stops.

Porno Drive-In, Knoxville, Tennesse

As we watch a tanned tight-bodied man and woman make it in a
hot tub, we try to ignore the young red-necks in the '74 Ford
pick-up also parked away from the screen who cut moonshine
with beer and go one by one into the bushes with a roll of toilet paper,
except when they press their faces against the window
on his side and yell, boy, got some for us?
Although we drive to the section of the lot farthest from them
we no longer feel safe. Your penis remains limp in my hand, my
vagina dry, no matter how much you rub my clitoris. We
straighten our clothes. You pick your afro. I switch on the car light
to put on lipstick and catch my face in the compact, my
white face, not the pink of the white boys, but the color inside
your palms. We squash ourselves into opposite sides of the car.

But soon we are sitting close. I nuzzle against your neck. We laugh
about the zebra-striped babies we would bring into the world
if we weren't careful and I retell the story of the Russian peasant
who murdered my great-grandmother Rivka, hung her
over the family clothesline and how I wished we could have made it
as if it never happened, that you could have carried her on your back,
helped to lower her gently in the narrow bed and handed me gauze,
until her wound was freckle-small and she returned from the dead
asking for a *glass tea* and a *bissel challah*. Again you pull me
into the story of the house-slave, your great-great-great grandmother
Adelaide, forced to lie with the master and how you wish
we could have broken into her master's bed chamber,
your hand over mine, as we cut the bastard's throat, freeing her forever.

Three Way Conversation

Adapted from the Ghinnawa form - Bedouin Oral Poetry

Your mother will never learn to drive.
She sees a scarf on the road and slams on the brakes.
Your father sees halos around the lamps along the highway.
A normal person would have his eyes examined. Not your father.

She never knows where to find a pot or a roll of toilet paper.
When she calls you, I dial the number.
Your father forgets how to get to places he always knew.
Thank God I can read maps.

Your mother's life consists of a series of questions
and the crossword puzzle.
Your father sits there eating canned pineapple not talking to me.
In no time at all he is asleep with his mouth open.

Since she broke her arm she is afraid to walk in the street,
but she has endless energy for department stores.
Do I have to collapse in front of him to make him believe I am not myself?
What kind of understanding can I expect
from a man who never vomited in his life.

Your mother really is a dirty fighter. Somehow it gets into every argument
that she had to work, while her friends worked for pin money.
Don't marry someone you have to take care of. When we were
newlyweds, I thought I could be your father's strength.

Your mother doesn't want to visit Max.
Of course she wouldn't go. It would make me too happy.
I finally gave in and invited Max, your father's only friend.
As usual your father was practically mute.

If she didn't start in, I wouldn't argue with her in front of company.
She is always rubbing my nose in something.
You should see how the other husbands treat their wives with kid gloves.
They know how lucky they are.

Continued

It's true I wanted another child. When you were tiny
I would hold your tusse in the palm of my hand.
When you were little you liked your father better.
He would sing to you "I'm a little teapot short and stout…"

You're always asking about our parents. If I hadn't sent my mother
to the nursing home she probably would still be alive.
I actually looked forward to talking to my mother every day
and living a few blocks away, strange as that may seem to you.

We should have never let you go to the therapist.
Don't you think you are old enough now to move back to New York?
You can't stand it, the way your father and I talk to each other?
Excuse me. I didn't realize you were so delicate.

Spilled Milk

I can still hear the clink
of the milk bottles he brought home
10:00 in the morning after he made
his deliveries for Bordens.
Thirty-five years, they never
gave him off a Jewish holiday.
The goy he asked to do his shift
on Yom Kippur refused and
the next day he dropped dead.
They called it a Jewish curse.
Then they stepped all over each other
to work for him.

What could I do after his stroke?
I put him in a nursing home.
He knows me, but can't talk anymore.
Fifty years we lived together
he would never weep in front of me.
Now all the time his eyes are tearing,
but there is no more Morris to cry.

Lovemaking wasn't so easy between us
in the early years. We both felt guilty.
We thought we weren't supposed to enjoy
it and I was always worried
about becoming pregnant.
Later on we worried the children would hear.
But after they grew up and moved out
and I couldn't bear anymore
we began to have fun.
It wasn't always before going to sleep either.
Sometimes during breakfast
he would say, *Let's go*
and roll his eyes up to the bedroom.
Luba, he would say, *I'll help you
take out the hairpins.*

Expanded/Extended Memory

You want to board that bus again
that nearly flies over back roads
to go where you will never be home,
the bus from Thessalaniki to Istanbul,
whose attendants amble down the aisle,
holding glass vials with rose smelling liquid.
You cup your hands together for the longest time,
not wanting to rub them against each other,
knowing that once you massage behind your ears
and the back of your neck
the tranquility will evaporate and become
worthless memory.
No matter how much embroidered,
memory can't eject you from behind the desk in Boston
where you are doing girlwork you despise,
looking into a screen with a blue background
and green spaces for data entry.
That clean-cut fraternity boy
doesn't seduce you, but you are broke
and need to use him.

The form says: MS DOS VERSION
                EXPANDED/EXTENDED MEMORY,

whatever that means,
as you process computer warranty agreements
sold to Los Alamos, Lodestar System, Occidental Petroleum,
men you vowed you would never
let touch you.

One Friday At The Katz's

Adelaide and I want straight hair. I set mine with
big juice cans. She wears a vinyl wig, hangs
it on the shower nozzle and quickly covers her kinky
grey hair before she washes out her cleaning rags.
We talk behind our hands. I wear metal braces and rubber
bands, she no teeth because she couldn't get her dentures
to fit and we both keep things from my mother her employer,
who is always giving us books, telling us school is the answer.
Adelaide wants to make my mother feel special, so she never
tells her about the other kids, sloppy as me, whose clothes
she picks off their bedroom floors and folds-up neatly, or
about the other women's houses, who unlike ours have two
sinks in the master bedroom and a gardener planting petunias in
the backyard. Because she doesn't want my mother
to feel sorry for her, she never discusses her neighborhood,
three buses away, where buildings with bricked-up windows
stand beside houses filled with people with nothing to do
but stare out the window. I don't want my mother to
worry about how hard it is for me to fit in, be smart or listen
to her and my father scream at each other: *you are my worst enemy.*

Today after school before Adelaide quits for the day
we say out loud what we already know about each other as
we eat brownies and cheese danish left for us: that I'll never
marry or have children and will only make things that no one
can use, but are beautiful to look at; and that she hopes it
won't be too long before she squirts her last white lady's
mirror with Windex and she'll be back to the cabin willed to her
by her mother in North Carolina, where she and her husband can
slaughter pigs, and in the heat of the afternoon he can play
poker with his pals, as she fans herself with a Chinese fan on
the porch, talking to neighbors as they stroll by like Mrs. Hill
whose fresh clothes sway on the line and Mrs. Washington
whose greens garden brings springtime.

Pick-Up Sticks

Barbara doesn't remember when she stopped believing what
she knew to be true. Maybe it was playing pick-up sticks on
linoleum in the room she shared with her big sister who grabbed a
bunch in one hand, let them fly every which way knocking over
the expensive lamp and didn't get punished for it, or when the
ketchup bottle fell out of her hand, or was it her sister's, splattering
glass and red globs.

But no matter how careful Barbara was, how much she concentrated
and was certain she picked one up without disturbing the others,
her sister would taunt, *You moved, you moved,* and her brother
would blame her for the bites on his arm. Barbara was positive she
had only pushed him, almost ... Maybe those teeth marks could be
hers. She imagined doing that and worse to him.

It couldn't be true. Her father had just wanted to wash her hair, although
before she got the training bra he only touched her with the back
of his hand. He said, *Take off your blouse, so it won't get wet.*
Then he started popping her bra straps, sticking his fingers
behind the clasp, moving them slowly towards the front. Barbara felt
somehow it was her fault. If she wasn't developing he would have
washed her hair until it was squeaky clean and kept the soap out of her
eyes.

As Barbara balances the bags of groceries on her knee and fumbles
with the key, she hears what sounds like two people scrambling,
the convertible shoved back into the sofa, big pillows hurled into place.
She kicks the door open. Donna from across the hall is smiling
awkwardly in the middle of the room. John offers Barbara
a beer, explaining, *Donna was just going. She came by
to invite us to a party.* Barbara walks past them into the kitchen to
slowly unpack things. Lining up the pork n' beans with the other
Campbell's cans, unwrapping the margarine and cramming it
into the refrigerator door, she thinks: a party, just what the doctor
ordered.

Army Brat

My mother died under a quack's knife trying to get a John's
baby out of her. I work the same crummy streets in Seoul's
Etaewon district she used to, before she met my father and
after he left her. He was tall as a poplar tree, black as the
place beyond the grave, and with one whack she'd be sailing
across the room. My mother married the G.I. I still have the
noregi that dangled from her satin *honbok* at the
wedding and the pair of wooden ducks. My mother was
proud to be a Dependent Wife. She wouldn't sit on
cushions, only high-backed chairs, nor have heat come up
through the floor like the peasants. She spoke to her
husband in English or was silent. He never learned Korean
and split before I was born. He thinks he is so great just
because he is American. I look too much like my father to
ever forget him or my mother's disgrace. Here, they pride
themselves on being of one bloodline, so marrying a
black ghost may be worse than turning tricks. Even
the Korean whores I work with talk to me in the familiar
form reserved for children and kitchen help.

When I am giving a Private a blow job, I think of the map
of Korea that they have embroidered on the back of
their satiny jackets, but sometimes I imagine a map with
silver and gold threads of the United States of America
where everybody is some mixture or other.

noregi (Korean) - hanging ornament worn with honbok, traditional Korean dress

A Tunnel Like Any Other

for Ben Schneberg

He has stood at the mouth of the tunnel
often but never entered.
He was sure its fangs would tear him apart
and his bloody strips of flesh would fuse
with the slime on its walls.
It would be blacker in there
than the bats flying out of his mouth
and more silent than his parent's house
in the middle of the night,
the only sound his screams
slamming against the walls
and slapping him across the face.

He knows the tunnel has no end.
But this time when his psychiatrist
tells him to try and says
he will wait on the other side,
the man pretends he is a rubber ball
that did not get caught
and rolls in there by mistake.

His stomach puffs out.
His heart beats
like when he lost his wife
in that huge department store,
but the tunnel doesn't chain him to stone
or cover his eyes with its black palms.
He feels sunlight on his face
and writes with a flourish on the wall,
This tunnel is like any other.

Fire In South Carolina

I'm running in woods.
Tiny yellow flowers are burning
and the charred tree limbs are blacker
than when I looked for them
when the moon kidnapped the sun.

No, I'm sleeping in my canopied bed,
white with gold trim
in the frail wooden house
as hydrangea crowd the lawn,
having no inkling that soon
their blue pompoms will burn.

Smoke not lilacs awakens me.
My eyes are watering. Maybe
grandma just left a pot on the stove.
Nothing bad can happen.

My girlfriends haven't begged
all the shopkeepers in town yet
to replace my sequined sweater
or the hard-backed copy of Jane Eyre;
and grandpa who whittled the cross
I still wear around my neck
hasn't gone back inside yet
to try to save grandma
whose doilies were straight-pinned
to every chair.

The Oral Tradition

His older sister's husband came home one night
drunk and bashed her head in and Naphtali found
her in a pool of blood when he returned for Shabbat
from his army stint. Naphtali didn't tell the woman
he told this story to, that he was sad and how
much he missed his sister. He said he wanted her
to stop asking questions and kiss him. She wanted
to catch his tears with her fingertips, the ones
that stayed inside his eyes, but instead she smeared
the plastic dome he never saw before with jelly.
He didn't like the smell and told her she shouldn't
worry, he would pull out just in time.

He always smoked a cigarette afterwards. Once
Naphtali told the woman about November,1982 in Lebanon
when a guy in his company captured by the "terrorists"
and brainwashed to believe he would die a
martyrs' death in their crazy holy war, drove a jeep
with a bomb directly into his own barracks, blowing
up the men who also slept with their
rifles, but not Naphtali, because he was with a woman
somewhere. As he tells this story, somehow tears run
down his face.

She tried to feel his sorrow, put her arms around his chest,
while he smoked another cigarette and mentioned
his baby sister was also dead. She had gone to
a doctor to check out if she was pregnant and was
anesthetized with something that killed her, but Naphtali
told the woman he did not want to talk about it
anymore. He wanted his tongue so deep inside her
he could feel her tonsils.

Pleasure Vehicle

In bed I empty our bathrobe pockets
of tiny compact cars,
replicas of autos we carpool in
and complain how Friday never comes,
to discover in their place
souvenirs of the Philippines—
jeeps MacArthur would never dream of.
Miniature jeepneys decorated like Mardi gras,
where circular mirrors, bicycle lights,
pink plastic fringe waving
from the top of antennae
adorn hoods painted with stylized wings
that look ready to fly off.

Open your bathrobe.
We are going to a party.
My fingers travel the overland route
across the chest, by way of the belly button
and across the penis
already extending its journey.

When Words Go On Vacation

This whole year you type words
wearing three-piece suits,
$100 words disgusted by
poems, hang-gliding, messages in bottles,
that know to march in line, in paragraphs
and fill-up white paper
until their numbers reach 1000.
They never pretend to be anything they are not.
The objects at their beck and call
become just like them and never dream
of masquerading:
the desk lamp as a pink flamingo,
the sharpened pencil as a dart
hurling to a bull's-eye.

But now they are on vacation,
taking a breather from breeding
in the collar of your starched button-down
and inside your silver cuff links
to invade the front of your rumpled orange t-shirt
with their new motto:
Every galosh is a glass slipper waiting to samba.

Collect Call From A Pay Phone In A Moan Olim

I

Conversation starts in safe territory.
She tells her father she read an article
about Beita Camp, the home
of a suspected terrorist,
his windowless cement box
bulldozed by the IDF.
Still inside, a torn picture of Arafat
tacked to the wall,
a pair of grimy jeans on a hook.
His small daughter standing outside.
The upside down V of her legs visible
through the thin nylon dress.
The daughter is hugging herself,
not crying or facing
the shell of the house,
but staring at Jaffa,
the home she has never seen,
but knows is surrounded by trees
bowing to Allah
laden with lemons and oranges.

Continued

II

She imagines that to get away from her mother
he has pulled the extension cord into the den
and is sitting on the over-stuffed leather sofa.
Her father says that the house is
very spiffy since the paint job,
even her room, the space she hasn't inhabited
for almost twenty years, but can never leave,
looks new. Like old times they begin to bicker.
He asks when she'll come home already.
When she'll stop running.

Maon Olim (Hebrew) - housing for new immigrants to Israel
IDF (English abbreviation) - Israeli Defense Force

I Could Die Now

If I were able to accomplish one task
with the skill of the pita seller
who slices through the streets
of Cairo crammed with cars
balancing a board on his head
high with pita
his arm reaching up to tug
with the genius of repetition
from the bottom of the pile
just the right round
the customer desires

Wedding In Beersheva

for Judy

Did I glimpse you out of the corner of my eye
floating above your son and his new bride
while they were carried on chairs
to the center of the circle
as a Chassid juggled kosher wine bottles?
Did I catch you for a split second leaping up
on your heavy legs, holding onto the arms
of your *frum* women friends in a rambunctious dance?
You looked as frumpy as ever, though greenish
and told me without moving your lips
that although I never married, had the mitzvah of children
or found G-d, you would rather be me
since I am not under ground.
You say you are sorry you did not make it to
your own unveiling, but you don't like rocks and platitudes
and two affairs in the same day is too much.
You have no time to find the right hat
to match the puce in your mother of the groom dress.

You won't believe that cancer was your dybbuk,
so here you are crashing the party.
This morning your husband crammed his pants pockets with pebbles
and wouldn't glance at his half of the headstone.
Tonight his sobs are *davening* silently behind his eyes,
and as much as he contorts his face
they won't keen and stream down his cheeks.
He can only guffaw and tear with laughter as
he hears you telling him: suck in the belly.

Suicide Note

for Louis Lingg (dead Nov. 10, 1887)

The day of the Haymarket Affair, making bombs with
Seliger in my small room, I was getting worked-up as we
talked about women exhausted over spinning machines
being fined for singing of their half-remembered villages,
fined for staying home to care for children stricken with
smallpox, and of the canary-dead coal miners obliged to buy
in the company store at 20% more than they would pay
outside. By evening there were fifty round and pipe-shaped
contrivances with caps attached and we celebrated the
virtues of dynamite! How cheerful and gratifying to light
the fuse in the neighborhood of a lot of rich loafers who
live off the sweat of other people's brows. A lb. of this stuff
beats a bushel of ballots. We quit the rooming house,
carrying between us by a stick through the handle a small
trunk filled with bombs which we left for safekeeping in
Zeph's Hall and went to take a beer in a saloon nearby,
when a bomb hurtled through the air, glowing and sputtering,
sadly not one of ours, striking down Degan and other foes
of the working man, changing the course of history.

I despise them, their order, their laws, their forced-propped
authority. I do not recognize the court's sentence. I am to
hang, not for a crime, but because I refuse to be governed
by the profit mongers, labor exploiters, children slayers,
home despoilers. I hear music from a ballroom. I wish I was
dancing with my girl. I hope when she presses her head
against another man's shoulder she will pretend sometimes
he is me smelling her perfume. Farewell, Adolf, Albert, August,
George. I will not follow you to the gallows to wear the noose
the plutocrats call justice. A comrade smuggled in a special
baby of a smoke, not exactly a Havana, but top quality never-
theless, inside a dynamite cartridge alive as the unborn in a
mother's womb. Certainly no time is better than the present
to sit back and inhale the aroma of a good 5 cent cigar.

Hang Gliding

*On Nov. 25, 1987, a member of Jibril's Popular Front
for the Liberation of Palestine crossed Israel's northern border.
He was captured and shot dead.*

I am sure he never heard of Otto Lilientahl
whose experiment with gliding broke his back,
but who said as he lay dying, *it was worth it*
for a moment to be a bird.
But for him, terrorist or hero,
whatever you call him, it was not about
wresting earth's stranglehold,
but a means to an end.

His air machine is light with cloth sails
and an engine that purrs like a moped's.
Its few pieces of metal show up
on a radar screen as merely a small dot.
Winds are favorable.
He knows it is just primitive enough to infiltrate
Israel's sophisticated anti-aircraft defenses.

He will walk through the front gate
of a base near Kiryat Shmona
armed with grenades, pistols,
machine guns and faith.

Wooden Bird

The wooden bird on my kitchen wall
that usually hangs
by its tail on nylon wire,
I hold in my lap and rub
as if it were Aladdin's lamp.
He carries me to the rickety bus
last year in Mexico
disappearing into hills
the color of adobe churches.
Night pushes through the window
and the woman sitting next to me
who wore three cages on her back
through the streets of Oaxaca,
a canary in each cage,
now sets them down
and covers them with black cloth.
She lowers her head in my lap
sensing I feel as weary.
In the morning, parting,
she gives me a cage, the canary singing.
But at the border it is taken from me.
The claws dig deep into a guard's shoulder
and what remains
is memory
deadwood carved to look like it chirps,
painted yellow as if it flies.

III

The Commuter Dreams Of Bertha

for Box Car Bertha

Bertha, let me come with you.
I'll travel light,
blanket roll on my back,
fry pan, stew pot, tin cup.
We'll flip the freight,
ride the rods and bumpers.
With luck we'll deck a passenger train
and go in style, lying down looking up
at sky blue as the swimming hole
we'll skinny-dip with other free lovers.
Beating our way from job to job, we'll
fling hash in Muncie,
empty bed pans in Sioux City,
seal envelopes and lick stamps in Boise,
model for art classes in Seattle,
bed down with *wob soap boxers*
until the springs are busted and
there's no more gin, then
we'll exchange their snores
for the train's hoot
and settle into a boxcar's cool corner.

But you rode your last rail long before I was born
and I'm the commuter who dozes off dreaming of you
every morning on the 7:08 out of South Station,
the wage slave who won't look out the window
at what she has stopped seeing.

Big Red

On the Trailways bus we are the sisters
we never had and open up about things
we would never tell in our our town
where it would be like renting an airplane
and writing our business in the sky.

We straggle into the Tomahawk Truck Stop
in Brush, Colorado knowing we look like
hell. Bringing her pencilled-in eyebrows together,
the waitress tells us we don't belong.

Even in the women's bathroom
we are not modest,
pull shirts over our heads,
reveal loose stomachs,
hangy breasts and share toothpaste.
Through white foam mouths
we brag about our cranky infants on
the tile floor who need diapering.

Back in the bus night creeps up like
a pickpocket over the strangled landscape,
making conversation a boulder pushed up hill.
In the long rolling dormitory we are no
longer we. In sleep, we each visit
our other family whose face we wear.

Biscuits

Mostly when I'm vacuuming the carpet
in Mr. Besdine's office
I don't worry, just do the work
and know I'll be sleeping in my own bed
when all the desks in all them offices
will have people sitting around them.
Sometimes I don't hear the vacuum cleaner
and I'm quiet like when I play
Praise God From Whom All Blessings Flow
in the Mission Baptist Church.
There are other times I imagine fixing biscuits
unrolling my cloth from the coffee can,
flour still on it from the last time,
smoothing it out on the counter,
cloth white, flour white.
My mother's biscuit cutter
made from an old Pet Milk can,
not a tack of rust on it,
presses in easy as a body to a hammock.
Some like biscuits and gravy,
I myself fancy biscuits with my homemade
muscadine jelly that comes from the
muscadine grape that grows wild.

A Visit To The Bible Belt After Eight Years

I

The golden dome of the 1982 World's Fair still dwarfs the buildings of
Knoxville's minuscule downtown.

Fay, now a pillar of the community remains a cross between Blanche
Dubois and Gertude Stein, but does not hold literary soirees anymore
because she has no time, is too busy renovating the shell of an eight
bedroom Victorian that she hopes to turn into a bed and breakfast, and
staying up all night with a sous-chef who looks like a giant version of the
Pillsbury Doughboy.

Kerry, the fabric artist who organized the kudzu festival to celebrate the
vine's capacity to grow anywhere, who was moving to Atlanta when she
last saw her, married a local boy, has a plump, curly haired daughter and
one in her stomach.

No one sees J.B. anymore; he edited the Hard Knoxville Review when she
started the poetry series, because his wife Monique keeps him to herself,
lets him out only to sing his poems with his post-punk band down at
Sullivan's Saloon. They say J.B. has become quite a celebrity.

As for Gary Tipton, they hoped she wouldn't ask, but they knew she
would, since they had been tight and all. They would break it to her
slowly and start newsy. Old Town? It used to be such a dive when you
and Gary hung there. Now it is the happening place. You didn't know
that Gary had bought a house with four working fireplaces and an oval
stained glass window in the vestibule. But they did not tell her then

Gary was dead. That the AIDS clinic down the block was torched the
same week the Tipton family decided to include their son's George Barber
House with the Queen Anne trim in the Fourth & Gill Open House Tour
draped in black, because Gary would have wanted it that way.

Continued

II

When she showed up for her HIV appointment at the Red Cross in
Kenmore Square near the home of the Boston Red Sox, she was told she
could pay cash to protect her anonymity and that her chances were good
that she was not infected even if he died of AIDS, because although they
were intimate and unprotected, their sexual contact was limited and the
year was 1981.

The nurse told her her veins were skinny and drew the blood with baby
needles, while she heard Gary say, *You're perfect. If you were only a man I
would marry you tomorrow* and remembered how they had loved to walk in
Old Town by the train tracks next to the abandoned brick factory topped
with towers and turrets, and talk how if they had a windfall they would
turn the area into another Soho, but she was angry that he let their
friendship die way before he lost control of his bodily functions and that
his memory couldn't just be filed away neatly with others of the Knoxville
years.

Now she has to worry that their brief dalliance could kill her. Eight years
later, the panes no longer fall out of the John Hancock building in
Boston, the town she has come to call home. Now she counsels people
not to kill themselves, and the poetry manuscript she diligently sends out
continues to find no publisher. She has had a number of lovers, but no
husband, will soon be too old to have a baby and keeps extra-strength
condoms in her purse.

A Thousand And One Nights

Usually when she put him in the liquor cabinet
and took the bottles into the bedroom,
she let him out an hour later.
He hated her slopping tongue in his ear,
her kissing him smack on the lips
when she smelled worse than
what he left in his diapers,
but he liked it when they rested
in the big bed
his small hand holding her thumb.

Then one day he wailed way past dinner time,
his chest shook, his eyes shut tight in his face,
until his crying became tearless,
his yelling without sound.
He doesn't remember how
he got out and found her
on the floor next to the bed
her eyes open like a doll's.
When he tells me the story,
he says he made it up.
But when we make love,
he plunges in so deep
his whole body is an umbrella
collapsing in on itself and
I hold him tighter than my mother
ever held me, while he moans,
I'm so alone…so alone.

Other Side Of The Coin

when he popped strawberries
whole into her mouth
she felt pain in her thighs
as if she were squatting down picking them

when he pressed hard against her
she wished he were an iron
smoothing her dress
while she was sitting
in the newly reupholstered armchair
watching him

when they quarreled she imagined
his mouth embracing one nipple then the other,
now that he has left her
she wants him back so she can pretend
she is living alone

July Silk Market

(Bursa, Turkey)

This time it is not thunder or a jet boom,
but a dish slipping out of my hand
crashing to the floor that may stop
your spinning the thread
with no lump or rough place.
I carried your eggs in a cloth
next to my skin and sewed cotton bags
into the clothing of my children
to hatch in their heat.
Silkworms, I am sorry.
I know your preference for silence
or the lilt of your own voices like rain
hitting aluminum pails left on roofs
everywhere in our village.

Please, I beg of you, don't stop singing.
Tomorrow morning I journey to the market,
the back of my black pick-up overfull
with mounds of white cocoons and will
pass by barely visible in the new light
squat mulberry trees emptied of leaves.

Note To My Japanese Lover

I wish I had the lacquerware writing box.
Its black lid sprinkled with golden flakes
for stars and ferns and the carriage
that whisked Yugao away
to her rendezvous with Genji.
But in the deserted mansion
during the night the spirits
jealous of their love
turned her body cold,
before she could touch him.

The inkstick skims water
in the inkstone's well
and rubs against stone
for ink blacker than your hair;
ink flows through bristles
of bamboo brush to kiss rice paper
with its moist black tongue,
so I with the hand of Ikyuu
may write of my longing.

A courier presents you my poem
attached to a sprig of cherry blossom:

The Great Ocean separates us.
My hands try to keep busy.
I wear my hair down.

Expatriate

I

Approaching the kiln
that climbed over mountains,
he wanted to run away.
Instead his father pulled him closer
as the flames' orange scarves curled
around the pots making them strong containers,
but he saw only himself tiny and weak
in the bottom of the teabowl
forever crawling up the curve
and sliding down.

II

He who was expected to be the eleventh
master grew older and sat during *Cha-no-you*
staring into the teabowl's chartreuse foam
wishing it were the ocean,
pretending he was in harmony
with the moment and the other guests,
as he imagined hurling the bowl
against rice paper walls,
the tea, green blood.

III

In New York City he never took out his kimono
and made pots that wouldn't bow,
save face or keep quiet,
pots that acknowledged no ancestors
only their maker who punched their walls outward
and left his knuckles.

Continued

IV

Yet most nights he dreams
he is not dreaming and is in Sasebo
on tatami his breath full,
legs underneath not aching,
placing in the *hana-ire*
the white hazel flower
he picked a moment ago
still dewy from the field.

My Father Leaves The Hospital Wearing his Yellow Shirt

Tkhines are prayers in Yiddish primarily recited by women.
It was the woman's domain to make candles for Yom Kippur.

If it were Yom Kippur eve and I did believe,
I would rub wax over one cotton thread,
then another and another,
for the threads of family members who died,
for the threads of the ones I only heard about,
for the ones whose stories are also dust;
and combine those of the few family members still alive,
with the threads of friends who are family and
the threads of strangers I wish were friends;
I would twist them all into one firm wick
and embed it in tallow.

They took a vein out of my father's leg,
put it in his chest to give the blood
a new path to follow.

G-d, please let him sleep tonight,
and in the morning
open his eyes wide.

Conch Republic

There our language was steam stroking tin roofs,
night-blooming cereus that opened
while we made love,
droopy vermilion cone-shaped buds
with banana fingers growing upward. Near

coral reefs where words were
pieces of eight and emeralds
we plunged into aquamarine waters,
our black flippered feet becoming the tails
of flame scallops and blue tangs. But

on that last Sunday thinking in our own
disparate languages of home and work we hid
behind our eyes and refused to tell each other
a word for Sunday or Monday
where salt water is something
one gargles for sore throat. Hooked

in the mouth by our countries
where we would have never spoken
we attack our separate mounds of newspaper,
too disenchanted to open
the massive dictionary between us.

Staying Put

I want to feel good staying put
like the woman who makes rope
in the mountains near Baguio
She has never left her village
and spins fine strands together
to make rope so long
it could wind around
the village ten times
Soon she will climb up the rope
to heaven
Her daughter who knows
the secret of the rope
has a daughter
whose small fingers are
learning to braid hair